SALSAS & DIPS

OVER 100 RECIPES FOR THE PERFECT
APPETIZERS, DIPPABLES, AND CRUDITÉS

SALSAS & DIPS

OVER 100 RECIPES FOR THE PERFECT APPETIZERS, DIPPABLES, AND CRUDITÉS

MAMIE FENNIMORE

CIDER MILL PRESS

BOOK PUBLISHERS

Contents

Introduction

Salsas and dips are essential when it comes to hosting get-togethers with family and friends all-year-round.
For as long as I can remember, my family has been in charge of the appetizers at any party. No matter how many different kinds of appetizers I have attempted to make, I always revert back to salsas and dips. For both, the recipes remain simple and the outcome always exceptional. Hence why I make them and why I now have these recipes. Sometimes, bringing the appetizers can seem like a daunting task. Most guests come to a party hungry and excited to see what apps are offered. Your dish is the first to be consumed and the first to be discussed. Yes, this may be stressful, as it's always been for me, but not to worry! The recipes in this book cover all your bases: hot, cold, fresh, cheesy, vegetarian, meaty, and even the sweet stuff.

Salsa

Salsa comes in many different styles: mild, spicy, smoky, citrusy, fruity, fresh, tomato based, not tomato based, etc. The term *salsa* traditionally means "sauce," which holds true to its use today. The salsas laid out in this book are the perfect sauces to dip a tortilla chip into or to top your favorite taco, nachos, salad, grilled steak, or chicken. It is important to use high-quality ingredients when creating a fresh salsa—you want those flavors to burst on everyone's taste buds! These recipes have a reputation, and I'm excited to finally share the secret to my salsa success.

Classic Tomato Salsa

ACTIVE TIME: 5 MINUTES • TOTAL TIME: 7 MINUTES • SERVING SIZE: 8 CUPS

If there's one salsa to make from this book, it's this one. Combining canned and fresh tomatoes is the key to the perfect consistency. It's fresh, flavorful, and will impress!

Mix everything together in a large bowl, garnish with cilantro, and serve with tortilla chips!

> EIGHT CUPS OF SALSA IS A LOT OF SALSA. SO, IF YOU ARE MAKING THIS FOR A SMALL GROUP, TRY CUTTING THE RECIPE IN HALF.

INGREDIENTS:

1 head garlic, minced

1 bunch fresh cilantro, chopped

4 cans crushed tomatoes (low sodium)

6 fresh tomatoes, diced

2 yellow onions, diced

$\frac{1}{3}$ cup juice from canned or jarred jalapeños

6 pickled jalapeños, seeded and minced

2 fresh jalapeños, seeded, diced

1 teaspoon sea salt

1 teaspoon fresh ground black pepper

Black Bean and Corn Salsa

ACTIVE TIME: 10 MINUTES • TOTAL TIME: 15 MINUTES • SERVING SIZE: 2 CUPS

There is no better way to use fresh summer corn than in this salsa. Use it to brighten up your next taco dinner.

INGREDIENTS:

2 ears corn, cooked and removed from cob

1 teaspoon sugar (optional)

1 can black beans, drained and rinsed

1 can diced tomatoes

1 fresh tomato, diced

1 bunch fresh cilantro, chopped

1 fresh jalapeño, finely chopped

1 medium shallot, finely minced

2 limes, juiced

1 tablespoon extra virgin olive oil

1 teaspoon sea salt

1 teaspoon freshly ground black pepper

1 To cook the corn, bring a large pot of water to a boil. Add 1 teaspoon of sugar to water if so desired (this adds a touch of sweetness to underripe corn). Place corn into boiling water and cover.

2 Let corn boil for 2–3 minutes then turn the heat off and keep covered. Let sit for 5 more minutes and remove from water.

3 Once cool enough to handle, cut the corn off the cob. Toss together corn, black beans, tomatoes, cilantro, jalapeño, and shallot. Dress with lime juice, olive oil, salt, and pepper. Serve with your favorite chips or tacos!

Ann's Corn Salsa

My grandmother Ann stuffs this delightful mixture into scooped-out tomatoes or red peppers. It's a fun way to serve this salsa as a side dish for dinner.

Toss all ingredients in a bowl and let chill in the fridge. Serve inside a scooped-out tomato or red pepper as a salad, or serve with tortilla chips.

INGREDIENTS:

2 ears corn, cooked and removed from cob

1 tablespoon chopped red onion

½ fresh green bell pepper, chopped

½ fresh red bell pepper, chopped

½ teaspoon sea salt

½ peeled, seeded English cucumber, chopped

½ fresh zucchini, diced

1 small jalapeño pepper, deseeded and finely chopped

1 medium tomato, deseeded and chopped

2 tablespoons apple cider vinegar

6 tablespoons extra virgin olive oil

1 teaspoon sea salt

1 teaspoon freshly ground black pepper

1 clove garlic, made into paste

Fresh parsley, for garnish

Tomatillo Salsa

ACTIVE TIME: 7 MINUTES • TOTAL TIME: 40 MINUTES • SERVING SIZE: 2–3 CUPS

Tomatillos are not, in fact, underripe red tomatoes. This relative of the tomato plant has a tart and herbal flavor that is just asking to be charred and turned into salsa. A touch of sugar helps balance the tart quality.

INGREDIENTS:

1 pound fresh tomatillos

1 tablespoon vegetable oil

1 teaspoon salt

1 teaspoon sea salt

¼ teaspoon sugar

1 small yellow onion

1 jalapeño pepper

½ cup fresh cilantro

1 lime, juiced

2 tablespoons extra virgin olive oil

1 Turn broiler on to 500 degrees Fahrenheit.

2 Peel tomatillos and place half on baking sheet. Toss with vegetable oil and salt. Broil until browned all over.

3 Take out and let cool slightly. Once cooled, place in food processor and process until smooth. Add the other half of raw, peeled tomatillos. Place the rest of the ingredients into the food processor. Mix until well combined and there are no large chunks.

4 Place in serving dish and let chill for 30 minutes. Serve on tacos, skewers, or with chips.

Variation: Add an avocado for a creamier version.

Roasted Tomato Salsa

ACTIVE TIME: 10 MINUTES • TOTAL TIME: 25 MINUTES • SERVING SIZE: 1½–2 CUPS

Roasting the tomatoes brings out a candy-like sweetness that adds depth of flavor to this salsa. The contrast of the roasted tomatoes and the fresh ingredients makes for an excellent addition to any grilled poultry or red meat.

1 Heat broiler to 500 degrees Fahrenheit. Broil tomatoes, jalapeños, and onions until browned and cooked through. You will need to toss them around once or twice during the broil. This will take about 7–10 minutes.

2 Remove from oven and let cool slightly. Once cooled, place all ingredients into a food processor and mix until combined. There should be no large chunks. Serve with tacos or tortilla chips.

INGREDIENTS:

1½ pounds ripe tomatoes

3 fresh jalapeños

½ small white onion, sliced

¼ cup water

½ cup chopped fresh cilantro, loosely packed

1 teaspoon sea salt

2 teaspoons apple cider vinegar

1 teaspoon freshly ground black pepper

Pineapple Salsa

Use this bright and refreshing salsa to top fish tacos or steak fajitas.

INGREDIENTS:

2½ cups fresh pineapple, diced (1 pineapple)

½ red onion, minced

3 fresh tomatoes, deseeded and chopped

2 jalapeños, deseeded and finely chopped

1 cup fresh cilantro, chopped

2 limes, juiced

2 tablespoons extra virgin olive oil

1 teaspoon sea salt

1 teaspoon freshly ground black pepper

Toss all ingredients in a bowl and serve.

Mango Salsa

I love to pair this tropical salsa with grilled swordfish or mahi mahi. Impressive enough for special occasions, and simple enough for a weeknight meal.

Toss all ingredients in a bowl and serve over grilled tuna or swordfish steaks. This is a summer staple for me!

Variation: Substitute with fresh peaches for a different stone fruit salsa.

INGREDIENTS:

1 ripe mango, peeled and diced

½ English cucumber, diced

1 cup fresh cilantro, chopped

1 shallot, minced

1 jalapeño, finely chopped

1 lime, seeded and juiced

1 tablespoon extra virgin olive oil

1 teaspoon sea salt

1 teaspoon freshly ground black pepper

Pico De Gallo

This literally means "beak of rooster." It does not have as much liquid as most other salsas, making it easier to use for a topping.

INGREDIENTS:

1 pound fresh plum tomatoes, diced

½ white onion, diced

½ cup fresh cilantro, chopped

¼ teaspoon garlic powder

1 lime, juiced

1 Serrano pepper, finely chopped

Toss all ingredients in a bowl and serve.

Chipotle and Adobo Salsa

Chipotles in adobo are simply smoked and dried jalapeño peppers packed in a sweet and sour sauce. This is a versatile ingredient that I always have stocked in my pantry.

Place all ingredients in a blender. Blend until well combined while leaving some small chunks.

INGREDIENTS:

1 pound fresh tomatoes

½ yellow onion, diced

3 chipotles in adobo, finely chopped

1 tablespoon adobo sauce

1 teaspoon sea salt

1 teaspoon freshly ground black pepper

1 cup fresh cilantro, chopped

Jicama and Apple Salsa

Jicama is a root vegetable originating in Mexico. This crisp and refreshing vegetable is like a cross between an apple, a potato, and a turnip. It's savory and nutty while still maintaining a clean tart taste. This salsa will definitely be the talk of the party!

INGREDIENTS:

1 jicama, peeled and diced

1 honey crisp apple, diced

1 lemon, juiced

½ orange, juiced

½ cup fresh cilantro, chopped

1 teaspoon freshly ground black pepper

1 teaspoon sea salt

½ teaspoon chili powder

1 shallot, minced

½ English cucumber, diced

Toss all ingredients in a bowl and serve.

Strawberry Salsa

Strawberries in a salsa?! Yes. Taste it to believe it.

Toss all ingredients in a bowl and serve.

INGREDIENTS:

1 pint fresh strawberries, diced

½ cup fresh cilantro, chopped

¼ cup fresh mint, chopped

1 shallot, minced

½ English cucumber, diced

1 jalapeño pepper, finely chopped

Cucumber Salsa

ACTIVE TIME: 10 MINUTES • TOTAL TIME: 10 MINUTES • SERVING SIZE: 2¼ CUPS

Enjoy this cool cucumber salsa in the height of the summer. I toss this with fresh greens or kale for an extra flavorful salad.

INGREDIENTS:

1 English cucumber, diced

½ red onion, finely chopped

1 cup fresh cilantro, chopped

¼ cup fresh mint, chopped

2 jalapeños, deseeded and chopped

2 limes, juiced

1 teaspoon sea salt

1 teaspoon freshly ground black pepper

1 teaspoon red chili flakes

2 tablespoons grapeseed oil

Toss all ingredients in a bowl and serve.

Radish Salsa

Radishes are for more than just decoration on a vegetable platter. Their peppery and crisp character makes for a perfect base to this fresh salsa.

Toss all ingredients in a bowl and serve.

INGREDIENTS:

1 bunch fresh radishes, diced

1 cup fresh cilantro, chopped

4 scallions, chopped

2 limes, juiced

1 teaspoon sea salt

1 teaspoon freshly ground black pepper

½ fresh pear, diced

Watermelon Salsa

This salsa is inspired by having far too much left over watermelon—those things are gigantic! Toss this salsa over grilled tuna steaks, rare of course.

INGREDIENTS:

2 cups watermelon, diced

½ cup fresh tomato, diced

2 limes, zested and juiced

1 teaspoon sea salt

1 teaspoon freshly ground black pepper

1 tablespoon extra virgin olive oil

1 teaspoon red chili flakes

Toss all ingredients in a bowl and serve with tortilla chips, on tacos, or on a salad.

Shishito Pepper Salsa

ACTIVE TIME: 15 MINUTES • TOTAL TIME: 25 MINUTES • SERVING SIZE: 1½ CUPS

Shishito peppers have finally broken into the farmers' market sphere. You never know if the one you take a bite out of will be spicy or mild. Either way, they are sublime when grilled.

1 To cook shishitos, skewer them and grill until blistered on the outside. Let cool.

2 Chop blackened peppers and toss with the rest of the ingredients. Serve with chips or over grilled meat.

INGREDIENTS:

1 pound fresh shishito peppers

1 teaspoon salt

1 teaspoon freshly ground black pepper

¼ cup sherry wine vinegar

¼ cup extra virgin olive oil

1 clove garlic, grated

Dips

Whether it's a large party or an intimate gathering, serving a dip can save you a ton of time and energy. These dip recipes can easily be cut in half or doubled with no problem, and there's one fit for every season! Try the guacamole recipes at the height of summer, the spicy red pepper dip in the crisp autumn air, the soul-warming Swiss fondue during a winter snowstorm, or the bright green cilantro-jalapeño hummus to awaken your tastebuds at the first sign of spring. As for the hot bean dip—well, serve that during bean dip season! When that is, is up to you, but in my opinion it's every day!

Classic Guacamole

ACTIVE TIME: 10 MINUTES • TOTAL TIME: 10 MINUTES • SERVING SIZE: 2–3 CUPS

This guacamole is my claim to fame. It's for all those who have ever asked what my recipe is! My favorite way to eat it is with a spoon...

1 Scoop out the avocados and place into mixing bowl. Gently mash the avocados while still leaving large pieces.

2 Add all remaining ingredients and stir together until well combined.

3 Dollop into a serving bowl and top with fresh cilantro leaves and a squeeze of fresh lime to prevent browning. Serve with tortilla chips, on your favorite tacos, or just grab a spoon!

INGREDIENTS:

4 ripe Haas avocados

1/3 medium red onion, diced

1 fresh jalapeño, deseeded and diced

1 bunch fresh cilantro, chopped (reserve a few leaves for garnish)

1 tablespoon extra virgin olive oil

1/4 cup fresh lime juice (juice of 1–2 limes)

1½ teaspoons sea salt

1 teaspoon freshly ground black pepper

Italian Guacamole

Here is a new Italian spin on the classic. Perfect for a party where there are no tortilla chips in sight! Serve with crostini or salty crackers.

INGREDIENTS:

4 ripe Haas avocados

⅓ medium yellow onion, diced

1 fresh Serrano chili, deseeded and diced

1 bunch fresh Italian parsley, chopped (reserve a few leaves for garnish)

1 tablespoon extra virgin olive oil

¼ cup fresh lemon juice (juice of 1–2 lemons)

¼ fresh tomatoes, chopped

1 clove fresh garlic, grated

1½ teaspoons sea salt

1 teaspoon freshly ground black pepper

1 Scoop out the avocados and place into mixing bowl. Gently mash the avocados while still leaving large pieces.

2 Add all remaining ingredients and stir together until well combined.

3 Dollop into a serving bowl and top with fresh lemon juice and a few sprigs of Italian parsley.

Guacamole with Grapes and Pomegranate

ACTIVE TIME: 10 MINUTES • TOTAL TIME: 10 MINUTES • SERVING SIZE: 2–3 CUPS

A true star! This guacamole will impress with its pop of color from the pomegranate and the subtle sweetness of the grapes. This will be a crowd favorite.

1 Scoop out the avocados and place into mixing bowl. Gently mash the avocados while still leaving large pieces.

2 Add all remaining ingredients and stir together until well combined.

3 Dollop into a serving bowl and top with fresh lemon juice and a sprinkle of pomegranate seeds.

INGREDIENTS:

4 ripe Haas avocados

⅓ medium red onion, diced

1 fresh jalapeño, deseeded and diced

1 bunch fresh cilantro, chopped (reserve a few leaves for garnish)

1 tablespoon extra virgin olive oil

¼ cup fresh lemon juice (juice of 1–2 lemons)

1 cup fresh seedless green grapes, halved (reserve a few for garnish) *red grapes are fine

The seeds of 1 pomegranate (reserve 1 tablespoon for garnish)

1½ teaspoons sea salt

1 teaspoon freshly ground black pepper

Avocado Smash

ACTIVE TIME: 5 MINUTES • TOTAL TIME: 5 MINUTES • SERVING SIZE: 1½ CUPS

Avocado toast? This is the recipe for that ever present menu item. It's delightful on freshly grilled Italian bread.

INGREDIENTS:

Scoop out avocados and place in a bowl. Add the rest of the ingredients and mash to desired consistency. Serve on toasted Italian bread for a delicious snack.

Avocado Crema

Drizzle over tacos or enchiladas for a yummy, creamy topping!

Put all ingredients in a food processor and mix until smooth. Scrape down sides once or twice. Place in bowl and serve.

INGREDIENTS:

1 ripe Haas avocado

⅓ cup sour cream

1 lime, juiced

1 teaspoon sea salt

1 teaspoon freshly ground black pepper

⅛ teaspoon chili powder

½ cup fresh cilantro, chopped

Homemade Sour Cream

ACTIVE TIME: 2 MINUTES • TOTAL TIME: 24 HOURS • SERVING SIZE: 1 CUP

Ever wonder how sour cream is made? Here it is. Yes, it's much more time effective to buy store-bought, but why not try it out and see if it's worth the wait!

INGREDIENTS:

2–3 tablespoons lemon juice

¼ cup whole milk

1 cup of heavy cream

Combine the ingredients. Cover with a secured paper towel and let sit at room temperature overnight until you have sour cream.

Spicy Sour Cream

I serve this version of sour cream exclusively at taco parties.

Use homemade or store-bought sour cream and stir in the juice of one lime and chili powder.

INGREDIENTS:

1 cup sour cream

¼ cup freshly squeezed lime juice

½ teaspoon chili powder

Chipotle and Adobo Crema

ACTIVE TIME: 3 MINUTES • TOTAL TIME: 3 MINUTES • SERVING SIZE: 1 CUP

Spread this tangy, smoky sauce on veggie burgers for added flavor. This sauce is addicting.

INGREDIENTS:

½ cup plain Greek yogurt

1 tablespoon tomato paste

1 tablespoon adobo sauce

chipotles in adobo, finely chopped

1 tablespoon honey

Mix all ingredients together in a bowl until well combined. Add more chipotle or honey to taste. Dip your favorite veggie burger, pita chips, or crudité in this flavorful sauce.

7-Layer Dip

This classic party dip is popular for a reason. There are 7 whole layers to hit every taste bud. You can't walk away from this one dissatisfied.

1 Combine the tomatoes, scallions, and cilantro in a small bowl. This will be the top layer.

2 Start with the refried beans as the bottom layer, then add the following layers in order: sour cream, salsa, black beans, guacamole, cheese, and top with the tomato mixture. Chill and serve.

INGREDIENTS:

1 cup tomatoes, diced

3 scallions, chopped

1 cup fresh cilantro, chopped

1 can refried beans

8 oz sour cream

1 jar salsa

1 can black beans

1 cup guacamole

1 cup shredded Mexican cheese

Artichoke Dip

ACTIVE TIME: 5 MINUTES • TOTAL TIME: 35 MINUTES • SERVES 6–8 PEOPLE

Warm and savory, this artichoke dip is a great fall or winter option. Enjoy on large Wheat Thins™ or sliced French bread.

INGREDIENTS:

1 can artichoke hearts, drained and chopped

¾ cup mayonnaise

1 cup Parmesan, grated

1 teaspoon Worcestershire sauce

1 clove garlic, grated

⅛ teaspoon cayenne pepper

1 Pulse all ingredients in a food processor until coarsely chopped and combined.

2 Pour mixture into an oven-safe baking dish and bake at 375 degrees Fahrenheit for 25–30 minutes or until lightly brown on top.

Hot Crab Dip

"Aunt Sally's Crab Dip" is one of the many names for this appetizer. It's a staple at Christmas, Thanksgiving, Fourth of July, Easter, you get the point . . . This recipe was one of the main reasons for compiling this reference.

1 Place cream cheese in a microwave-safe bowl and microwave for 30–45 seconds until soft but not melted. Then add the drained crab and all other ingredients (except for slivered almonds). Mix until combined.

2 Put in oven-safe baking dish and sprinkle slivered almonds on the top. Bake at 400 degrees Fahrenheit for 20–25 minutes or until top is golden brown and dip is hot all the way through.

3 Remove from oven and let cool for 5–10 minutes. Then serve with saltines!

INGREDIENTS:

1 stick cream cheese

1 can of crab packed in water, drained

⅓ cup sour cream

2 tablespoons horseradish

1 tablespoon Worcestershire sauce

2 teaspoons Tabasco

½ cup slivered almonds

Cold Spinach Dip

Serve this chilled dip inside of a pumpernickel bread bowl. There is nothing better than eating the serving dish.

INGREDIENTS:

1 package frozen spinach, defrosted and squeezed of all excess liquid

8 oz sour cream

½ cup mayonnaise

1 packet vegetable soup mix (Knorr, Lipton, etc.)

Red pepper flakes for garnish

1 Chop spinach. Mix all ingredients in bowl until well combined.

2 Let sit for an hour or overnight to soften the dried vegetables. Serve with pumpernickel bread, sourdough, and crudité.

Sour Cream and Onion Dip

This is best served on football Sundays with an extra-large bag of potato chips. It's tasty and it's no secret that everyone loves it. A favorite amongst my dad and his friends!

Mix all ingredients in a bowl until well combined. Serve with potato chips and vegetables.

INGREDIENTS:

8 oz sour cream

1 packet French onion soup (Lipton or Knorr)

¼ teaspoon cayenne pepper

Frank's Buffalo Chicken Dip

ACTIVE TIME: 5 MINUTES • TOTAL TIME: 30 MINUTES • SERVES 6–8 PEOPLE

My brother, Frank, lives on this dip. It's spicy, creamy, full of chicken, and topped with a ton of melted cheese. There is truly nothing better!

INGREDIENTS:

1 stick cream cheese

¾ cup blue cheese dressing

1 cup cooked, shredded chicken (more or less to your liking)

1 cup Frank's RedHot sauce (or more to your liking)

1 cup shredded Mexican cheese (or enough to lightly cover the top of the dip)

1 Place cream cheese in a microwave safe bowl and microwave for 30–45 seconds until soft but not melted. Stir in the blue cheese dressing, chicken, and hot sauce. Mix until combined.

2 Pour mixture into an oven-safe baking dish and top with shredded cheese. Bake at 425 degrees Fahrenheit for 20–25 minutes or until cheese is melted and lightly browned.

3 Remove from oven and let cool for 5–10 minutes. Then serve with tortilla chips!

Ando's Hot Bean Dip

This bean dip is legendary in my family. Make it once and your life will change for the better. I must credit this one-of-a-kind dip to La & Andy!

1 Put half of both cheeses on the bottom of the baking dish. Mix cream cheese, sour cream, salsa, and refried beans until combined and smooth.

2 Pour into baking dish on top of cheese. Sprinkle top of mixture with the rest of the shredded cheese. Bake at 350 degrees Fahrenheit for 20–30 minutes or until cheese is golden brown and sides are bubbling. Serve with tortilla chips!

INGREDIENTS:

8 oz shredded cheddar

8 oz Monterey Jack

8 oz cream cheese

8 oz sour cream

¼ cup jarred salsa

1 can refried beans

½ packet taco seasoning

Cold Bean Dip

ACTIVE TIME: 10 MINUTES • TOTAL TIME: 10 MINUTES • SERVES 6–8 PEOPLE

When it's too hot for hot bean dip, try this chilled version. It's refreshing and flavorful. Perfect for a day on the porch or a summer party.

INGREDIENTS:

- ½ cup sour cream
- lime juice
- can refried beans
- 1 cup shredded Mexican cheese
- jalapeños, sliced for garnish

Mix together sour cream, lime juice, and refried beans until well combined.

Place in serving dish and top with Mexican cheese and jalapeños. Chill. Serve with chips and salsa.

Chicken Liver Mousse

This recipe might seem like a stretch for beginners in the kitchen, but don't be afraid! It's a lot easier than it seems. Be sure not to overcook the livers or they will be tough and chewy. This is a great dip if you want to change things up in your appetizer rotation.

1 Cook chicken livers in half of the butter for 5 minutes. Then add onions and cook until translucent (5–7 mins).

2 Deglaze pan with Madeira. Let cool slightly.

3 Place cooked livers, remaining half of the butter, and the rest of the ingredients in a food processor. Process until mostly smooth. Scrape down the sides of machine once or twice during process.

4 Place into serving dish and top with a few fresh sprigs of thyme. Serve with crostini.

INGREDIENTS:

1 pound chicken livers

1 stick butter (salted or unsalted)

1 large yellow onion, diced

3 tablespoons Madeira

2 hard-boiled eggs

3 tablespoons fresh Italian parsley, chopped

1 teaspoon fresh thyme, minced

1 teaspoon sea salt

1 teaspoon freshly ground black pepper

$\frac{1}{8}$ teaspoon cayenne pepper

Dried Beef Dip

ACTIVE TIME: 10 MINUTES • TOTAL TIME: 40 MINUTES • SERVES 6–8 PEOPLE

A Philadelphia special here and a favorite of mine! This decadent dip is best served with extra-large Fritos.

INGREDIENTS:

8 oz cream cheese

2 3-oz packets dried beef, chopped (or 6 oz dried beef from butcher)

¼ green bell pepper, finely diced

¼ red bell pepper, finely diced

½ medium yellow onion, finely chopped

½ cup sour cream

½ teaspoon garlic salt, or to taste

½ teaspoon freshly ground black pepper

1 Mix all ingredients in a bowl until well combined.

2 Place in baking dish and bake at 350 degrees Fahrenheit for 20–30 minutes or until you see browning and bubbles around the edges. Serve with large Fritos and veggies!

I've searched and searched for the best store-bought hummus, but absolutely nothing compares to the homemade version. It's simple, flavorful, and you can adjust it to your own liking. This is pure chickpea hummus!

1 Place all ingredients in a food processor and blend until relatively smooth. Consistency is really up to you! I like my hummus with a little bit of texture. If it is too thick, feel free to add a tablespoon of tap water.

2 Dollop hummus into a serving dish and top with a drizzle of extra virgin olive oil. Serve with warm pita triangles, pita crisps, and crudité.

INGREDIENTS:

2 cans chickpeas (garbanzo beans)

¼ cup tahini (sesame paste)

¾ cup fresh lemon juice (the juice of 3 lemons)

¾ cup extra virgin olive oil

2 teaspoons sea salt

1 tablespoon freshly ground black pepper

1 teaspoon Tabasco

FOR BEST RESULTS LET HUMMUS SIT IN THE REFRIGERATOR FOR AN HOUR OR TWO, AND THE FLAVORS WILL DEVELOP EVEN MORE!

Cilantro-Jalapeño Hummus

ACTIVE TIME: 10 MINUTES • TOTAL TIME: 10 MINUTES • SERVING SIZE: 2–2½ CUPS

This green hummus is colorful, clean, and full of complementary flavors. This recipe was originally just cilantro-lime until my brother Harry tossed a whole jalapeño in . . . we've never gone back! But if spice isn't your thing, simply remove the hot peppers, and enjoy.

INGREDIENTS:

2 cans chickpeas (garbanzo beans)

¼ cup tahini (sesame paste)

¾ cup fresh lime juice (the juice of 3 limes)

¾ cup extra virgin olive oil

2 teaspoons sea salt

1 tablespoon freshly ground black pepper

1 teaspoon Tabasco

1 bunch fresh cilantro roughly chopped (save a few leaves for garnish)

2 fresh jalapeños, seeded and roughly chopped

1 Place all ingredients in a food processor and blend until relatively smooth. Consistency is really up to you! I like my hummus with a little bit of texture. If it is too thick, feel free to add a tablespoon of tap water.

2 Dollop hummus into a serving dish and top with a few fresh cilantro leaves. Serve with warm pita triangles, pita crisps, and crudité.

FOR BEST RESULTS LET HUMMUS SIT IN THE REFRIGERATOR FOR AN HOUR OR TWO, AND THE FLAVORS WILL DEVELOP EVEN MORE!

FOR BEST RESULTS LET HUMMUS SIT IN THE REFRIGERATOR FOR AN HOUR OR TWO, AND THE FLAVORS WILL DEVELOP EVEN MORE!

Roasted Red Pepper Hummus

ACTIVE TIME: 15 MINUTES • TOTAL TIME: 45 MINUTES • SERVING SIZE: 2–2½ CUPS

I like to make this hummus along with the cilantro-jalapeño and classic lemon for a perfect trio.

1 To roast a red bell pepper, start by washing and drying the pepper. Then on the grill, under the broiler, or right on the open flame of your stove top, roast the pepper until the skin is black. It will look burnt, but bear with me!

2 Once charred all around, place the pepper in a brown paper bag, close it, and let it rest for 20 minutes to 1 hour. The steam created in the sealed bag will loosen the skins from the meat of the pepper. Remove the pepper from the bag and peel off the charred skin. It is fine if there is a little bit of char that remains. It's flavor!

3 Remove the seeds from the inside of the pepper and discard. Roughly chop the pepper.

4 Place all ingredients in a food processor and blend until relatively smooth. Consistency is really up to you! I like my hummus with a little bit of texture. If it is too thick, feel free to add a tablespoon of tap water.

5 Dollop hummus into a serving dish and top with a drizzle of extra virgin olive oil and a sprinkle of fresh feta cheese if you have it on hand. Serve with warm pita triangles, pita crisps, and crudité.

INGREDIENTS:

1 red bell pepper, roasted, deseeded and roughly chopped (see prep in instructions)

2 cans chickpeas (garbanzo beans)

¼ cup tahini (sesame paste)

¾ cup fresh lemon juice (juice of 3 lemons)

¾ cup extra virgin olive oil

2 teaspoons sea salt

1 tablespoon freshly ground black pepper

1 teaspoon Tabasco

Garlic and Cumin Hummus

ACTIVE TIME: 10 MINUTES • TOTAL TIME: 10 MINUTES • SERVING SIZE: 2 CUPS

This one is for the garlic lovers. It's packed full of fresh garlic flavor with a hint of smokiness from the cumin.

INGREDIENTS:

2 cans chickpeas (garbanzo beans)

½ cup tahini (sesame paste)

¾ cup fresh lemon juice (juice of 3 lemons)

½ cup extra virgin olive oil

2 teaspoons sea salt

1 teaspoon ground cumin

3 cloves fresh garlic, grated

1 tablespoon freshly ground black pepper

1 teaspoon water (if needed)

1 Place all ingredients in a food processor and blend until relatively smooth. Consistency is really up to you! I like my hummus with a little bit of texture. If it is too thick, feel free to add a tablespoon of tap water.

2 Dollop hummus into a serving dish and top with a drizzle of extra virgin olive oil and some freshly cracked black pepper. Serve with warm pita triangles, pita crisps, and crudité.

White Bean Hummus

ACTIVE TIME: 10 MINUTES • TOTAL TIME: 10 MINUTES • SERVING SIZE: 2–2½ CUPS

Cannellini beans (white beans) can also make for a stellar hummus. They are rich and creamy with even more fiber and protein than the chickpea! If you like a smooth, silky texture for your hummus then try out this recipe.

1 Place all ingredients in a food processor and blend until relatively smooth. Consistency is really up to you! I like my hummus with a little bit of texture. If it is too thick, feel free to add a tablespoon of tap water.

2 Dollop hummus into a serving dish and top with a few pieces of freshly diced tomatoes and a drizzle of olive oil. Serve with warm pita triangles, pita crisps, and crudité.

INGREDIENTS:

2 cans white beans (cannellini beans)

¼ cup tahini (sesame paste)

¾ cup fresh lemon juice (juice of 3 lemons)

¾ cup extra virgin olive oil, plus 1 tablespoon for garnish

2 teaspoons sea salt

1 tablespoon freshly ground black pepper

1 teaspoon Tabasco

3 sprigs flat leaf Italian parsley for garnish

½ fresh tomato, diced for garnish

Black Bean Hummus

ACTIVE TIME: 10 MINUTES • TOTAL TIME: 10 MINUTES • SERVING SIZE: 2 CUPS

Serve this hummus with tortilla chips at your next gathering! It's also great to use in a burrito or on a taco, like the way you would use refried beans.

INGREDIENTS:

2 cans black beans

¼ cup tahini (sesame paste)

¾ cup fresh lime juice (the juice of 3 limes)

¾ cup extra virgin olive oil

2 teaspoons sea salt

1 tablespoon freshly ground black pepper

1 teaspoon Tabasco

1 teaspoon anchovy paste

1 Place all ingredients in a food processor and blend until relatively smooth. Consistency is really up to you! I like my hummus with a little bit of texture. If it is too thick, feel free to add a tablespoon of tap water.

2 Dollop hummus into a serving dish and top with a few fresh cilantro leaves. Serve with warm pita triangles, pita crisps, and crudité.

Edamame Hummus

ACTIVE TIME: 10 MINUTES • TOTAL TIME: 10 MINUTES • SERVING SIZE: 3–4 CUPS

Edamame is simply a soybean that has not fully matured. These beans are packed with nutrients and full of flavor. They are fantastic on their own, but why not make hummus out of them?

1 Place all ingredients in a food processor and blend until relatively smooth. Consistency is really up to you! I like my hummus with a little bit of texture. If it is too thick, feel free to add a tablespoon of tap water.

2 Dollop hummus into a serving dish and top with a few crumbled seaweed crackers and a drizzle of olive oil. Serve with seaweed crackers, warm pita, and crudité.

Variation: To make an edamame hummus with wasabi variation, simply add wasabi powder or wasabi paste.

INGREDIENTS:

4 cups edamame beans (frozen)

¼ cup tahini (sesame paste)

¾ cup fresh lemon juice (the juice of 3 lemons)

¾ cup extra virgin olive oil

2 tablespoons low sodium soy sauce

2 teaspoons sea salt

1 tablespoon freshly ground black pepper

1 teaspoon Tabasco

Olive Hummus

ACTIVE TIME: 10 MINUTES • TOTAL TIME: 10 MINUTES • SERVING SIZE: 2–2½ CUPS

Why not combine two Mediterranean classics like fresh olives and hummus? This salty delight is best topped with a generous crumbling of feta cheese.

INGREDIENTS:

2 cans chickpeas (garbanzo beans)

½ cup mixed olives, pitted

¼ cup tahini (sesame paste)

¾ cup fresh lemon juice (the juice of 3 lemons)

¾ cup extra virgin olive oil

2 teaspoons sea salt

1 tablespoon freshly ground black pepper

1 teaspoon Tabasco

1 Place all ingredients in a food processor and blend until relatively smooth. Consistency is really up to you! I like my hummus with a little bit of texture. If it is too thick, feel free to add a tablespoon of tap water.

2 Dollop hummus into a serving dish and top with a few chopped olives. Serve with warm pita triangles, pita crisps, and crudité.

Kalamata Olive Tapenade

ACTIVE TIME: 10 MINUTES • TOTAL TIME: 10 MINUTES • SERVING SIZE: 1½–2 CUPS

Originating from the south of France, better known as Provence, tapenade is an olive and caper spread used as an appetizer on crostini, or sometimes spread on top of grilled meat, poultry, and fish.

Place all ingredients into food processor and pulse until well combined. Do not over process to a paste. Serve with pita chips, on crostini, or with fresh vegetables.

Variation: Mix this recipe up with two different olive variations:

To make a green olive tapenade variation, use Spanish green olives.

To make a red olive tapenade variation, use Spanish red olives, and ¼ cup sun-dried tomatoes.

INGREDIENTS:

2 cups Kalamata olives or Nicoise olives, pitted

¼ cup extra virgin olive oil

1 tablespoon capers, drained

2 anchovy fillets or 1 tablespoon anchovy paste

1 clove fresh garlic, grated

¼ cup fresh basil

1 teaspoon fresh thyme

¼ cup Italian flat leaf parsley

1 teaspoon fresh oregano

1 lemon, juiced

Sun-Dried Tomatoes and Pistachio Tapenade

ACTIVE TIME: 15 MINUTES • TOTAL TIME: 20 MINUTES • SERVING SIZE: 1½–2 CUPS

Sun-dried tomatoes are a true godsend. They might be my favorite kind of candy! Combine them with pistachios in this dip, and the result will be a real winner.

INGREDIENTS:

1 shallot, minced

¼ cup extra virgin olive oil

1 teaspoon dry vermouth

¾ cup sun-dried tomatoes packed in oil

½ cup pistachios, shelled

½ cup flat leaf Italian parsley, chopped

1 teaspoon fresh thyme, minced

½ lemon, zested and juiced

1 teaspoon sea salt

1 teaspoon freshly ground black pepper

1 Cook shallot in 1 tablespoon of the olive oil for 3–5 minutes until lightly brown.

2 Deglaze pan with vermouth. Let cool.

3 Toss all ingredients into food processor. Mix until well combined. There should not be any large chunks. Serve on crostini or enjoy with vegetables. If too thick, add some water.

Spinach Artichoke Dip

Simple. Warm. Decadent. Enjoy this at your next party or save it all for yourself for a delicious dinner.

1 Pulse all ingredients in a food processor until coarsely chopped and combined.

2 Pour mixture into an oven-safe baking dish, and bake at 375 degrees Fahrenheit for 25–30 minutes, or until lightly brown on top.

INGREDIENTS:

1 can artichoke hearts, drained and chopped

1 8 oz package frozen spinach, defrosted and squeezed of all excess liquid

¾ cup mayonnaise

1 cup Parmesan, grated

1 teaspoon Worcestershire sauce

1 clove garlic, grated

⅛ teaspoon cayenne pepper

Hot Spinach Dip

Using frozen spinach for these kinds of dips makes the process ten times easier. Less to cook, less to clean. More time to eat!

INGREDIENTS:

1 tablespoon olive oil

1 yellow onion, minced

1 clove garlic, minced

1 package frozen spinach, defrosted and squeezed of all excess liquid

½ cup whole milk

8 oz cream cheese

½ cup shredded mozzarella cheese

2 teaspoons Worcestershire sauce

1 teaspoon Tabasco

1 teaspoon freshly ground black pepper

1 teaspoon sea salt

1 Heat oil in pan and cook onion and garlic until translucent. Then add spinach to warm through.

2 Over low heat, add milk. Cook until milk is warm, then add cream cheese and mozzarella, stirring continuously. Add the rest of the ingredients.

3 Pour mixture into baking dish and bake at 400 degrees Fahrenheit for 25–30 minutes or until golden brown and bubbly on top.

Variation: Add 1 cup shredded chicken, or 1 cup lump crab meat for variations.

Cold Crab Dip

Stuff this dip into mini bell peppers and endive leaves for an added crunch. It's a great way to present this delectable crab dip. It looks fancy too!

Whisk together cream cheese, lemon juice, and sour cream until well combined. Add all other ingredients and mix together.

Garnish with a light sprinkle of Old Bay and a few sprigs of fresh parsley. Serve with saltines and vegetables.

INGREDIENTS:

- 8 oz cream cheese
- 1 lemon, juiced
- ¼ cup sour cream
- 1 cup lump crabmeat, or 1 can crab packed in water
- 3 scallions, finely chopped
- 1 tablespoon Worcestershire sauce
- 1 teaspoon Tabasco
- 1 teaspoon Old Bay seasoning

Buffalo Cauliflower Dip

ACTIVE TIME: 15 MINUTES • TOTAL TIME: 40–45 MINUTES • SERVES 6–8 PEOPLE

For the vegetarians out there, here is the solution to your buffalo chicken dip dilemma. It's just as tasty with cauliflower!

INGREDIENTS:

1 large head cooked cauliflower, finely chopped

8 oz bar cream cheese

¾ cup blue cheese dressing

1 cup Frank's hot sauce

2 cups shredded Mexican cheese

1 To cook cauliflower, bring ½ inch of water to a boil. Add chopped cauliflower florets. Cover and cook for 4–6 minutes or until tender. Let cool slightly.

2 Microwave cream cheese for 30–45 seconds or until slightly softened. Add blue cheese and hot sauce and stir until well combined. Gently fold in cauliflower.

3 Put into baking dish and top with shredded cheese. Bake at 400 degrees Fahrenheit for 20–25 minutes or until cheese is slightly golden. Serve with tortilla chips or celery!

BLT Dip

Extra bacon after breakfast? Repurpose it in this fun take on the BLT.

1 Mix together sour cream and cream cheese until well combined. Fold in the bacon, onion, tomatoes, and pepper.

2 Make a bowl out of the lettuce leaves and pour dip into lettuce bowl. Top with extra bacon crumbles. Serve with toast points.

INGREDIENTS:

8 oz sour cream

4 oz cream cheese

8 slices bacon, cooked and diced (save a few crumbles for garnish)

1 small yellow onion, diced

2 medium tomatoes, diced

2 teaspoons freshly ground black pepper

5 large lettuce leaves

Yellow Queso

Warm, gooey cheese is the key to any fiesta.

INGREDIENTS:

1 Heat half and half in a skillet over medium low heat. Once warmed through, start slowly whisking in the cheeses. Keep mixing until melted.

2 Then stir in the rest of the ingredients. Serve immediately with chips!

White Queso

Fontina is an Italian cheese made from cow's milk. It's mild but has nice grassy and nutty flavors, especially in the summertime when the cows are eating the freshest grass! It adds an extra layer of complexity to this version of queso.

1 Heat half and half to a low simmer. Slowly add cheeses while stirring constantly. Add rest of ingredients and stir until well combined.

2 Place into serving dish and top with garnishes. Enjoy while hot and gooey!

INGREDIENTS:

1 cup half and half

12 oz American cheese (make sure this is high-quality cheese)

5 oz fontina cheese

¼ cup pickled jalapeños, diced

1 small can green and red chilis

Pinch of fresh grated nutmeg

A few dashes of Tabasco

½ teaspoon chili powder

½ teaspoon sea salt

1 teaspoon freshly ground black pepper

1 fresh jalapeño, sliced into rings for garnish

1 tomato, deseeded and chopped for garnish

Fresh cilantro for garnish

Beer Cheese

Beer and cheese are meant to be paired together. This recipe combines them into one simple dip. Make sure to save an extra beer to drink with it!

INGREDIENTS:

8 oz sharp cheddar cheese (yellow or white)

8 oz cheddar cheese (yellow or white)

2 cloves garlic, grated on microplane

1 teaspoon mustard powder

⅛ teaspoon cayenne pepper

½ teaspoon sea salt

½ teaspoon freshly ground black pepper

1½ tablespoons Worcestershire sauce

1 teaspoon Tabasco

8 oz your favorite pilsner, amber ale, or any flavorful beer

A few fresh chives, finely chopped for garnish

1 Place all ingredients, except beer and chives, in food processor. Pulse until chopped and blended.

2 With machine on, stream in the beer. Mix until smooth.

3 Place in serving dish, sprinkle top with chives, and serve with your favorite chips and veggies.

Variation: Spread between two pieces of bread to make a beer grilled cheese!

Swiss Fondue

ACTIVE TIME: 10 MINUTES • TOTAL TIME: 15 MINUTES • SERVES 4–6 PEOPLE

Swiss fondue is what solidified my life's dedication to cheese and wine. It's savory, gooey, sweet, and not to mention easy!

1 Heat 1 tablespoon of butter in medium nonstick pan. Heat garlic and shallot slightly and add both cheeses, wine, and vermouth.

2 Once cheese begins to melt, add the rest of the ingredients and cook gently until cheese is completely melted and everything is mixed in. Do not cook too long.

3 Serve immediately with bread cubes and fresh vegetables.

INGREDIENTS:

1 tablespoon butter

½ clove garlic, grated

1 shallot, minced

1 pound Gruyere cheese

½ pound Swiss cheese, like Emmental

1 cup dry white wine (white burgundy, Pinot Grigio)

2 tablespoons dry vermouth

1 tablespoon cornstarch

½ lemon, juiced

$\frac{1}{8}$ teaspoon freshly grated nutmeg

1 teaspoon freshly ground black pepper

Whipped Ricotta Dip

This is a great dip if you are scrambling before a party.
It takes five minutes and there are very few ingredients!
My sister, Grace, suggested I add fresh herbs to this dip,
and from there comes all the herb variations!

INGREDIENTS:

1 lb ricotta cheese
1 lemon, juiced
1 teaspoon freshly ground black pepper
¼ cup extra virgin olive oil

Whisk all ingredients in a bowl until whipped.
Serve with crostini.

Variation: Here are two of my favorite
herb variations:

Add basil and parsley for a variation.
Garnish with a few chopped cherry tomatoes.

Or, make a lemon and herbes de Provence
variation. Zest the lemon before juicing. Add
zest. Add 1 teaspoon herbes de Provence.
Garnish with a few sprigs of fresh thyme.

Whipped Blue Cheese Dip

Honey and blue cheese are a match made in heaven. This salty-sweet combo is great as an appetizer, or even dessert. The floral character of the honey is a perfect complement to the earthy blue cheese.

1 Whisk all ingredients in a bowl until well combined and fluffy.

2 Place into serving dish and top with a light drizzle of honey. Serve with crostini and vegetables, or spread on a hamburger!

INGREDIENTS:

1 cup blue cheese

1 teaspoon freshly ground black pepper

1 tablespoon whole milk

1 teaspoon honey

Whipped Feta Dip

ACTIVE TIME: 5 MINUTES • TOTAL TIME: 5 MINUTES • SERVES 4-6 PEOPLE

Salty and spicy, this dip is perfect to go alongside grilled lamb chops, or spread on grilled bread.

INGREDIENTS:

2 cups fresh feta

1 tablespoon extra virgin olive oil

2 tablespoons freshly squeezed lemon juice

1 teaspoon freshly ground black pepper

½ teaspoon red chili flakes

Place all ingredients in a food processor and process until mixed and fluffy!

Variation: Add grilled scallions for a variation.

Whipped Goat Cheese Dip

ACTIVE TIME: 5 MINUTES • TOTAL TIME: 5 MINUTES • SERVES 6–8 PEOPLE

Goat cheese is tangy and grassy. A touch of honey helps to balance out the flavors.

Place ingredients in a food processor and blend until whipped and smooth. Serve with crostini and roasted red peppers or crudité.

Variation: This recipe is a great base for delicious variations. A few of my favorites:

• Add 1 teaspoon fresh thyme for an added touch of flavor.

• Add 2 teaspoons of herbes de Provence for a Provençal spin.

• Add 1 fresh beet, finely chopped, for a pink variation!

INGREDIENTS:

16 oz fresh goat cheese

1 teaspoon white wine vinegar

1 tablespoon extra virgin olive oil

1 teaspoon freshly ground black pepper

1 teaspoon honey

Baked Goat Cheese Dip with Honey Drizzle

ACTIVE TIME: 10 MINUTES • TOTAL TIME: 30 MINUTES • SERVES 6–8 PEOPLE

The tangy goat cheese in this recipe mellows out in the oven to make for a light, airy, and delicate dip.

INGREDIENTS:

16 oz fresh goat cheese

1 teaspoon white wine vinegar

1 tablespoon extra virgin olive oil

1 teaspoon freshly ground black pepper

1 teaspoon honey

4 oz cream cheese

1 tablespoon chopped chives

1 Place ingredients in a food processor and blend until whipped and smooth.

2 Put into baking dish, and bake at 400 degrees Fahrenheit for 15–20 minutes until top is golden and bubbly.

3 Top with chopped, fresh cherry tomatoes or chopped roasted red peppers. Serve with crostini.

Deviled Egg Dip

If you don't have one of those trays that hold your deviled eggs in place, this is the dip for you. It packs all the punch of a deviled egg, but in a simple dip that's easy to transport.

To boil eggs, place eggs in saucepan and cover with water. Bring to rapid boil, cover, and turn off heat. Let stand for 15 minutes. Then drain and run eggs under cool water. Remove shells from eggs and rinse eggs.

Roughly chop the eggs and put in food processor with the rest of the ingredients, except the paprika. Mix until smooth.

Place in serving dish and lightly dust top with paprika. Serve with toast points.

INGREDIENTS:

1 dozen fresh eggs

¾ cup mayonnaise

1 tablespoon Dijon mustard

½ teaspoon dry mustard

1 teaspoon Worcestershire sauce

⅛ teaspoon cayenne pepper

2 teaspoons sea salt

1 teaspoon freshly ground black pepper

Paprika to dust on top

Homemade Mustard

ACTIVE TIME: 5 MINUTES • TOTAL TIME: 48 HOURS • SERVING SIZE: ½ CUP–1 CUP

Serve this delightful mustard with soft pretzels and hot dogs, or spread it on a turkey sandwich.

INGREDIENTS:

¾ cup yellow mustard seeds

1 cup apple cider vinegar

⅔ cup water

2 teaspoons sea salt

1½ teaspoons cane sugar

1 Place seeds, vinegar, and water in a large bowl and let soak for two days.

2 Put soaked seeds, liquid, salt, and sugar into food processor. Process until smooth. If too thick, feel free to thin out to desired consistency with more water.

3 Serve with pretzels, mini hot dogs, sliders, etc.

Homemade Honey Mustard

ACTIVE TIME: 2 MINUTES • TOTAL TIME: 2 MINUTES • SERVING SIZE: ½ CUP

Experiment with different kinds of honey in this dip. I suggest clover, orange blossom, acacia, blueberry, or pine tree. See what flavor combo you like best!

Mix all ingredients in a bowl and serve with chicken nuggets.

INGREDIENTS:

½ cup Dijon mustard

2 tablespoons honey

½ teaspoon freshly ground black pepper

Homemade Ketchup

ACTIVE TIME: 1 HOUR • TOTAL TIME: 2–5 HOURS • SERVING SIZE: 2 CUPS

Serve at a BBQ with burgers, hot dogs, and grilled potatoes.

INGREDIENTS:

32 oz can whole tomatoes

1 yellow onion, finely chopped

2 tablespoons vegetable oil

½ cup apple cider vinegar

½ cup dark brown sugar

1 teaspoon garlic powder

1 teaspoon chili powder

¼ teaspoon freshly ground nutmeg

¼ teaspoon allspice

1 teaspoon paprika

2 tablespoons tomato paste

1 teaspoon sea salt

1 teaspoon freshly ground black pepper

⅛ teaspoon cayenne pepper

1 Place tomatoes in a food processor and purée until smooth. Meanwhile cook onion in vegetable oil until lightly browned.

2 Add tomato purée to onions and stir. Mix in the rest of the ingredients and mix until combined. Cook over low heat, stirring occasionally for 50 minutes to 1 hour. Sauce should be thick.

3 Once thickened, let cool. Pour into food processor and blend until smooth. Let chill in fridge for 2–5 hours and serve.

Homemade BBQ Sauce

ACTIVE TIME: 15 MINUTES • TOTAL TIME: 1 HOUR • SERVING SIZE: 4–4½ CUPS

Brush this sauce on chicken, ribs, brisket, or pulled pork.

1 Whisk all ingredients in a large saucepan. Bring the sauce to a boil, then reduce to simmer and let cook for about 45–50 minutes.

2 Once sauce is thickened to your desired consistency, serve!

INGREDIENTS:

2 cups ketchup

⅓ cup apple cider vinegar

1 teaspoon chili powder

1 teaspoon freshly ground black pepper

1 teaspoon sea salt

1 tablespoon tomato paste

¼ cup water

½ cup honey

1 tablespoon light brown sugar

1 tablespoon Worcestershire sauce

1 teaspoon dried thyme

2 teaspoons dried mustard

¼ teaspoon cayenne pepper

1 teaspoon garlic powder

1 teaspoon onion powder

2 teaspoons instant coffee grounds, or 1 tablespoon brewed coffee

¼ cup Coca-Cola

1 tablespoon low sodium soy sauce

Ranch Dipping Sauce

ACTIVE TIME: 10 MINUTES • TOTAL TIME: 10 MINUTES • SERVING SIZE: 1–1½ CUPS

Ranch doesn't always have to be made in the "hidden valley." Try making it at home and see how having "local" ranch amplifies the flavor of any veggie or salad.

INGREDIENTS:

½ cup buttermilk

¼ cup mayonnaise

½ cup sour cream

2 tablespoons fresh Italian parsley, chopped

2 tablespoons fresh chives, chopped

1 tablespoon apple cider vinegar

1 teaspoon sea salt

¼ teaspoon garlic powder

1 teaspoon freshly ground black pepper

3 dashes hot sauce

Whisk all ingredients in a bowl until well combined. Serve with fresh veggies, like any ranch lover would.

Blue Cheese Dipping Sauce

Try using this recipe in the buffalo chicken or cauliflower dip instead of store bought. Or use it on a hamburger!

Put all ingredients in a food processor and blend until smooth. Stir in some extra blue cheese crumbles for texture. Serve with buffalo wings, celery, and carrots.

INGREDIENTS:

¾ cup mayonnaise

¾ cup sour cream

2 tablespoons freshly squeezed lemon juice

1 tablespoon freshly ground black pepper

1 teaspoon sea salt

1 teaspoon Tabasco

1 cup Gorgonzola, Stilton, or any blue cheese (leave some to stir in at the end)

3 dashes Worcestershire sauce

Cocktail Sauce

If your shrimp were still kickin', they would be swimming in this sauce!

INGREDIENTS:

1 cup ketchup

1 tablespoon Sriracha

1 tablespoon chili garlic sauce

2 tablespoons lime juice

1 tablespoon horseradish

Mix everything in a bowl until combined. Serve with shrimp.

Fava Bean Dip

Fava bean dip is a staple on Greek dip samplers. It's creamy and mild, and pairs perfectly with a crisp Greek white wine like Moschofilero.

Place all ingredients in a food processor and combine until smooth. Put in serving dish and chill.

When ready to serve, drizzle top with extra virgin olive oil. Serve with warm pita and feta.

INGREDIENTS:

2 cups fava beans

1 clove garlic, grated

1 teaspoon sea salt

1 teaspoon freshly ground black pepper

1 lemon, juiced

1 cup extra virgin olive oil

Spicy Red Pepper and Feta Dip

ACTIVE TIME: 10 MINUTES • TOTAL TIME: 10 MINUTES • SERVING SIZE: 1–1½ CUPS

If spicy is not your thing then remove the cayenne pepper and chili flakes from this recipe, and you still have a beautiful red pepper dip! Another favorite of mine.

INGREDIENTS:

1 pound feta, crumbled

2 red bell peppers, deseeded

2 tablespoons freshly squeezed lemon juice

½ teaspoon cayenne pepper (or more to taste)

½ teaspoon freshly ground black pepper

½ teaspoon paprika

⅓ cup extra virgin olive oil

1 Place ingredients in food processor, except oil. While processing, drizzle oil into mixture. Process until smooth and whipped.

2 Put in serving dish and let sit in the fridge for an hour to allow the flavors to mingle. Serve with a drizzle of extra virgin olive oil and some chili flakes on top. Enjoy with pita and crudité.

Salmon Roe Dip

ACTIVE TIME: 10 MINUTES • TOTAL TIME: 10 MINUTES • SERVING SIZE: 1-1½ CUPS

Also known as Taramosalata, this Greek classic is salty and rich like the smoked or cured salmon you put on a bagel. Perfect for a light snack!

Soak bread in water and then squeeze out excess water. Place ingredients in food processor, except oil. While processing, drizzle in the oil until spread is smooth.

Place in serving dish and let chill for an hour to let flavors meld. Garnish with a few olives and parsley, and serve with warm pita and veggies.

INGREDIENTS:

10 oz (9-10 slices) stale white bread, crusts removed

3-4 oz fish roe (tarama)

2 lemons, juiced

1 small red onion, grated

¾ cup extra virgin olive oil

Baba Ganoush

ACTIVE TIME: 25–30 MINUTES • TOTAL TIME: 30–35 MINUTES • SERVING SIZE: 2 CUPS

Roasting the eggplant brings out the rich and smoky flavors in this dip. It's creamy with a nice fresh spark from the lemon juice.

INGREDIENTS:

3 medium eggplants

½ cup extra virgin olive oil

1 teaspoon sea salt

1 tablespoon tahini (sesame paste)

½ teaspoon chili powder

2 lemons, juiced

1 clove of garlic, grated

1 teaspoon freshly ground black pepper

1 Cut eggplants in half and poke holes all over with a fork. Toss with 1–2 tablespoons of olive oil and salt. Bake at 375 degrees Fahrenheit for 15–20 minutes, flesh side up. Eggplant is done when lightly brown and tender all the way through.

2 Remove from oven and let cool slightly. Once cool enough to handle, remove flesh from skins and discard skins. Put eggplant in food processor with the other ingredients and pulse until smooth with a few lumps.

3 Place in bowl and either serve immediately or let chill in fridge. Enjoy with warm pita, chips, and vegetables.

Garlic Dip

ACTIVE TIME: 45 MINUTES • TOTAL TIME: 1 HOUR • SERVING SIZE: 2 CUPS

Dip falafel or grilled veggies in this dish for a garlicky kick at your next vegetarian BBQ. It also goes great with grilled meats!

1 Clean and peel potatoes. Cut into one inch cubes. Boil for 30 minutes or until tender.

2 Put potatoes through food mill or ricer. Let cool.

3 Chop garlic, and use the back of the knife to make a paste. Put all ingredients (except potatoes) into food processor to make a paste.

4 Fold the paste into riced potatoes until smooth. Serve with pita and vegetables.

INGREDIENTS:

2 large russet potatoes, cooked

6 cloves fresh garlic, made into paste

½ cup extra virgin olive oil

½ cup water

2 lemons, juiced

²/₃ cup blanched almonds

2 tablespoons champagne vinegar

2 teaspoons sea salt

2 teaspoons freshly ground black pepper

Tzatziki

I love this refreshing dip to cool down any spicy food, or to cut the smokiness of grilled meats.

INGREDIENTS:

1 cup Greek yogurt

½ English cucumber, finely diced

1 clove garlic, grated

1 teaspoon sea salt

1 teaspoon freshly ground black pepper

3 tablespoons extra virgin olive oil

1 tablespoon red wine vinegar

1 tablespoon lemon juice

1 teaspoon fresh mint

Whisk all ingredients in a small bowl until the mixture is well combined. Garnish with a thin slice of cucumber and a mint leaf.

Smoked Salmon Dip

Perfect for Sunday brunch!

Place all ingredients in a food processor and combine until smooth. Put in serving dish and chill. Serve with a garnish of fresh parsley and bagel chips.

INGREDIENTS:

8 oz cream cheese

½ cup sour cream

1 lemon, juiced

1 teaspoon freshly ground black pepper

1 tablespoon horseradish

6 oz smoked salmon

2 teaspoons red onion, finely chopped

1 tablespoon capers, drained

Lentil Dip

ACTIVE TIME: 5 MINUTES • TOTAL TIME: 30–40 MINUTES • SERVING SIZE: 1½ CUPS

Lentils are quick and easy to make, and they take on whatever flavor you want. They are the perfect base to any dip.

INGREDIENTS:

1 cup dried lentils
3 cups water
1 tablespoon tahini
1 lemon, juiced
¼ cup extra virgin olive oil
1 teaspoon sea salt
2 teaspoons freshly ground black pepper
1 teaspoon coriander
3 cloves garlic

To cook lentils, boil water and add lentils to boiling water. Turn heat to low and let simmer until lentils are cooked through and all the water is absorbed, 20–30 minutes. Let cool.

Add all ingredients to a food processor and blend until smooth. Let chill in refrigerator for 1–2 hours and serve.

Lentil Avocado Dip

ACTIVE TIME: 5 MINUTES • TOTAL TIME: 30–40 MINUTES • SERVING SIZE: 1½ CUPS

Per usual, avocados make everything better.

1 To cook lentils, boil water and add lentils to boiling water. Turn heat to low and let simmer until lentils are cooked through and all the water is absorbed, 20–30 minutes. Let cool.

2 Add all ingredients to a food processor and blend until smooth. Let chill in refrigerator for 1–2 hours and serve.

INGREDIENTS:

1 cup dried lentils

2 cups water

1 ripe avocado

1 tablespoon tahini

2 limes, juiced

½ cup extra virgin olive oil

2 teaspoons sea salt

2 teaspoons freshly ground black pepper

1 teaspoon coriander

3 dashes Tabasco

Broccoli Cheddar Dip

Love broccoli cheddar soup in the winter? Spread the love at your next gathering with this cheesy delight.

INGREDIENTS:

1 head broccoli

16 oz shredded cheddar cheese

1 teaspoon freshly ground black pepper

½ stick cream cheese

1 cup sour cream

5 scallions, chopped

1 To cook broccoli, place into $\frac{1}{2}$ inch of boiling water and cover. Cook for 15 minutes. Let cool.

2 Place all ingredients into a food processor and blend until smooth. Serve with sourdough bread and veggies.

Raita

This Indian specialty is a necessity when I have Indian food. I didn't even know it existed until my Aunt Amy and Uncle John introduced me to this delightful sauce. It's cool and refreshing to help cut through the spices of your favorite dish.

Mix all ingredients in a bowl, and chill for an hour. Serve with veggies, crackers, or Indian food!

INGREDIENTS:

½ cup plain yogurt

½ English cucumber, deseeded and diced

¼ cup fresh cilantro, chopped

2 scallions, finely chopped

¼ teaspoon coriander

½ teaspoon sea salt

½ teaspoon freshly ground black pepper

Roasted Mushroom Dip

ACTIVE TIME: 5 MINUTES • TOTAL TIME: 40 MINUTES • SERVES 4–6 PEOPLE

Another great dip to share with your vegetarian friends!

INGREDIENTS:

1 pound of your favorite mushrooms

1 teaspoon sea salt

1 teaspoon freshly ground black pepper

2 tablespoons extra virgin olive oil

1 cup fontina cheese

2 teaspoons fresh thyme, chopped

½ cup fresh parsley, chopped

½ lemon, juiced

1 Toss together mushrooms, salt, pepper, and oil on a baking sheet. Bake at 425 degrees Fahrenheit for 20–30 minutes or until brown.

2 Top with cheese and thyme and bake for 5–7 more minutes.

3 Garnish with parsley and lemon, and serve with toast points.

Roasted Pumpkin Dip

Pumpkins are king in the fall and winter. They are sweet, savory, and perfect to enjoy by the fire. Serve this dip at your next cozy gathering.

1 To roast pumpkin, cut in half and brush with vegetable oil. Sprinkle with 1 teaspoon salt. Roast pumpkin at 425 degrees Fahrenheit for 25–30 minutes. Let cool.

2 Scrape flesh from skins and put in food processor. Add the rest of ingredients to the food processor and blend until smooth. Serve with pumpernickel crostini or water crackers. Perfect for the fall!

INGREDIENTS:

1 medium sugar (pie) pumpkin or butternut squash

1 tablespoon vegetable oil

2 teaspoons sea salt (1 for roasting, 1 for dip)

1 teaspoon freshly ground black pepper

¼ cup extra virgin olive oil

1 teaspoon fresh thyme

¼ teaspoon freshly ground nutmeg

¼ cup freshly grated Parmesan cheese

1 tablespoon freshly squeezed lemon juice

1 tablespoon plain Greek yogurt or sour cream

BBQ Chicken Dip

Bring this dip to this year's super bowl party!

INGREDIENTS:

Soften cream cheese in microwave for 30–45 seconds. Mix all ingredients, except cheese, in a bowl until well combined.

Place in baking dish and top with cheese. Bake at 400 degrees Fahrenheit for 20–25 minutes or until golden and bubbly.

Variation: Substitute chicken with pulled pork, shredded brisket, or red kidney beans for different variations.

Classic Bruschetta

Use the summer's bounty to make this fresh bruschetta. Toss in any garden herbs you're growing!

Toss all ingredients in a bowl and let chill for 30 minutes to an hour. Serve on top of toasted Italian bread, or serve on top of pasta.

INGREDIENTS:

3 tomatoes, diced

1 shallot, finely chopped

1 clove fresh garlic, minced

1 tablespoon fresh chives, chopped

1 teaspoon fresh thyme, minced

1 tablespoon extra virgin olive oil

1 tablespoon red wine vinegar

1 teaspoon sea salt

1 teaspoon freshly ground black pepper

Tomato Basil Bruschetta

ACTIVE TIME: 5 MINUTES • TOTAL TIME: 5 MINUTES • SERVING SIZE: 1–1½ CUPS

This is a fun take on the Caprese salad, and with this fresh appetizer there's no fork and knife necessary!

INGREDIENTS:

3–4 tomatoes, diced

1 cup fresh basil, thinly sliced

1 clove fresh garlic, minced

1 tablespoon extra virgin olive oil

2 teaspoons balsamic vinegar

¼ cup fresh mozzarella cheese, cubed

1 teaspoon sea salt

1 teaspoon freshly ground black pepper

Toss all ingredients in a bowl and serve on toasted Italian bread.

Bruschetta with Prosciutto

ACTIVE TIME: 5 MINUTES • TOTAL TIME: 5 MINUTES • SERVING SIZE: 1½–2 CUPS

Prosciutto is a cured and dried ham from Italy. It goes hand in hand with mozzarella cheese and fresh tomatoes in this bruschetta.

Toss all ingredients in a bowl and serve with toasted Italian bread.

INGREDIENTS:

3–4 fresh tomatoes, diced

1 shallot, minced

¼ sharp provolone cheese, cubed

6 prosciutto slices, chopped

½ cup fresh Italian parsley, chopped

1 tablespoon extra virgin olive oil

2 teaspoons white wine vinegar

1 teaspoon freshly ground black pepper

Collins' Spicy Jalapeño Corn Dip

ACTIVE TIME: 5 MINUTES • TOTAL TIME: 35 MINUTES • SERVES 6–8 PEOPLE

This dip is unforgettable–super decadent and equally as delicious. Use fresh summer corn when available, but frozen works great too when the summer bounty runs out.

INGREDIENTS:

8 oz cream cheese

24 oz corn

1 stick butter

⅓ cup sour cream

⅓ cup pickled jalapeños, chopped

2 tablespoons jalapeño juice

1 teaspoon garlic powder

Cherry tomatoes for garnish

1 Soften cream cheese and butter in microwave for 30–45 seconds. Add all other ingredients. Mix until combined.

2 Bake at 350 degrees Fahrenheit for 30 minutes or until golden and bubbly. Serve with tortilla chips.

Pizza Dip

This is a true crowd pleaser!

1 Soften cream cheese in microwave for 30–45 seconds. Mix with everything except 1 cup of mozzarella cheese and pepperoni. Pour mixture into baking dish and top with cheese and pepperoni.

2 Bake at 400 degrees Fahrenheit for 30–45 minutes or until golden brown. Serve with bread and tortilla chips.

INGREDIENTS:

8 oz cream cheese

2 cups mozzarella, shredded

½ cup Parmesan, freshly grated

½ cup cheddar cheese, shredded

2 teaspoons freshly ground black pepper

1 teaspoon fresh thyme, minced

1 teaspoon dried basil

1 cup marinara sauce

⅓ cup pepperoni, sliced

Authentic Cheesesteak Dip

ACTIVE TIME: 20 MINUTES • TOTAL TIME: 1 HOUR • SERVES 6–8 PEOPLE

The cheesesteak. As a Philadelphia native, I think I know a thing or two about it. The most important thing to know about the classic cheesesteak is absolutely NO peppers and mushrooms allowed. Only steak, cheese, and caramelized onions.

INGREDIENTS:

1 ribeye steak, very thinly sliced

8 oz cream cheese

¼ cup mayonnaise

1 onion, thinly sliced and caramelized

2 cups shredded mozzarella cheese (reserve 1 cup for top)

1 cup shredded provolone

1 teaspoon freshly ground black pepper

2 tablespoons olive oil

1 teaspoon garlic powder

Herbs for garnish

1 To cook the onions, heat up olive oil in a pan over medium heat. Toss in onions with salt and pepper, and slowly cook until caramelized. This should take about 15–20 minutes.

2 Add all ingredients into a bowl and mix until well combined.

3 Pour into baking dish and top with remaining cup of mozzarella. Bake at 400 degrees Fahrenheit for 25–30 minutes until golden brown.

Peanut Satay Dip

ACTIVE TIME: 10 MINUTES • TOTAL TIME: 10 MINUTES • SERVING SIZE: 1–1¼ CUPS

Peanuts, tangy, salty, and a perfect accompaniment for chicken skewers and kabobs.

Mix all ingredients in a bowl. Serve with chicken skewers or crudité.

        This can also be used as a Pad Thai sauce if thinned with pasta water.

INGREDIENTS:

- 1 cup creamy peanut butter
- 3 tablespoons rice wine vinegar
- ¼ cup low sodium soy sauce
- 1 tablespoon honey
- ½ cup boiling water
- 2 limes, juiced
- 1 red chili sauce
- freshly ground black pepper
- Handful of chopped peanuts for garnish

Ceviche

Traditionally found in coastal regions around the world, ceviche is raw fish cooked in citrus acid (lime, lemon, orange, grapefruit, etc.). Ceviche is fresh, clean, and flavorful. This dip is the perfect party appetizer, which everyone will rave about.

INGREDIENTS:

1 pound shrimp, or 1 pound ahi tuna, diced

5 limes, juiced

2 shallots, minced

½ English cucumber, diced

1 cup fresh cilantro, chopped

2 teaspoons sea salt

2 teaspoons freshly ground black pepper

Toss all ingredients in a bowl and let chill for 10–20 minutes. Serve with tortilla chips.

Variation: For variations, use fresh salmon, yellowtail, fluke, red snapper, ahi tuna, or lobster. Add 1 ripe avocado, diced, to any variation for a heartier take on this appetizer.

Dessert Dips

Dips are popular appetizers and generally quite easy to prepare. Why not take everything great about an appetizer dip and apply it to dessert? Having a dip for dessert cuts out the process of slicing up a cake or pie, scooping ice cream, you name it. Toss one of these sweet treats on the table and let everyone enjoy a fork- and spoon-free delight!

Marshmallow Fluff Dip

ACTIVE TIME: 5 MINUTES • TOTAL TIME: 5 MINUTES • SERVING SIZE: 1–1½ CUPS

Dip chocolate-covered graham crackers in this cloud-like dip for a whimsical take on campfire s'mores. If you have a kitchen torch, caramelize the top of the dip for a dramatic effect.

Mix all ingredients in a bowl and serve with cookies or fruit.

INGREDIENTS:

8 oz marshmallow fluff

4 oz cream cheese

1 cup powdered sugar

Greek Yogurt Dip

Fresh fruit and this dip are a made for each other. The nutmeg adds a little "je ne sais quoi."

INGREDIENTS:

1 cup plain Greek yogurt

¼ cup honey

½ teaspoon freshly ground nutmeg

⅛ teaspoon sea salt

Mix all ingredients in a bowl until well combined. Let chill. Serve with fruit.

Cool Whip

Get your strawberries ready!

1 Combine gelatin and water in small sauce pan. Simmer until gelatin is completely dissolved.

2 In a bowl, start whisking heavy cream until it begins to thicken. Add sugar and liquid gelatin. Whisk in rest of ingredients and beat until you have stiff peaks.

3 Let chill and serve with fresh strawberries.

INGREDIENTS:

2 teaspoons unflavored gelatin

½ cup water

2⅓ cups heavy cream

1 cup powdered sugar

2 teaspoons pure vanilla extract

Whipped Cream

Use this recipe to top pie, pound cake, ice cream, fresh fruit, you name it. Whipped cream is incredible easy to "whip up".

INGREDIENTS:

2 cups heavy whipping cream

1 teaspoon pure vanilla extract

Whisk until you have soft peaks. Be sure not to over mix or you will have butter. Let chill and serve!

Cookie Dough Dip

ACTIVE TIME: 10 MINUTES • TOTAL TIME: 10 MINUTES • SERVING SIZE: 1–2 CUPS

I love cookie dough, and love to snack on it when baking cookies. Here is an egg-free cookie dough recipe that you can serve as a dip!

1 Beat together cream cheese, butter, and sugars until fluffy. Add the salt and vanilla and mix until well combined.

2 Fold in mini chocolate chips and serve with graham crackers and fruit.

INGREDIENTS:

8 oz cream cheese

1 stick unsalted butter

½ cup powdered sugar

½ cup packed light brown sugar

½ teaspoon sea salt

½ teaspoon pure vanilla extract

1 ½ cups mini chocolate chips, semi-sweet

Peanut Butter Dip

Put this out at a party and watch it disappear instantly. Maybe have a backup bowl on hand . . .

INGREDIENTS:

4 oz cream cheese

1 cup smooth peanut butter

½ cup powdered sugar

1 tablespoon whole milk

½ cup mini chocolate chips, semi-sweet

1 Soften cream cheese and peanut butter in microwave for 20–30 seconds.

2 Beat together until well combined. Whisk in milk and powdered sugar until smooth.

3 Fold in chocolate chips and serve.

Candy Dip

Serve this candy dip at this year's Halloween party. You can use your favorite candy, and it will be a hit.

Beat together all ingredients, except M&Ms, until light and fluffy. Fold in M&Ms. Serve with pretzels and graham crackers.

Variation: For a variation, you can use any of your favorite candies. Try Snickers, Milky Way, 100 Grand, Twix, Heath bars, peanut M&Ms, etc.

INGREDIENTS:

8 oz cream cheese

½ cup powdered sugar

2 tablespoons whole milk

½ stick butter

½ teaspoon pure vanilla extract

1 cup mini M&Ms

Tiramisu Dip

I was never a huge fan of tiramisu for texture reasons. This recipe changed my mind, because the lady fingers are removed from the recipe and instead used as a crunchy dippable. Absolutely delicious!

INGREDIENTS:

1⅓ cups mascarpone cheese

½ cup fresh ricotta cheese

½ cup powdered sugar

1 teaspoon pure vanilla extract

2 tablespoons brewed espresso

1 teaspoon fine espresso powder

2 tablespoons Kahlua

1 teaspoon cocoa powder

½ cup semi-sweet chocolate, chopped

1 Beat together both cheeses, sugar, vanilla, brewed espresso, espresso powder, and Kahlua in a stand mixer until light and thoroughly combined.

2 Place in serving dish and dust top with cocoa powder and chopped chocolate. Let chill. Serve with ladyfingers, fruit, or pound cake.

Brownie Batter Dip

ACTIVE TIME: 5 MINUTES • TOTAL TIME: 5 MINUTES • SERVING SIZE: 1–1½ CUPS

Enjoy with pretzels and strawberries! It's chocolate heaven.

1 Soften cream cheese and butter in microwave for 20–30 seconds.

2 Beat softened cream cheese and softened butter in a bowl until creamed together. Add the rest of the ingredients and stir until very well combined. Serve with fresh fruit and pretzels.

INGREDIENTS:

8 oz cream cheese or plain Greek yogurt

1 stick butter

1½ cups powdered sugar

½ cup cocoa powder

2 tablespoons brown sugar

⅓ cup whole milk

1 teaspoon vanilla extract

½ teaspoon sea salt

Pumpkin Spice Dip

Serve inside of a pumpkin for an even more impressive presentation!

INGREDIENTS:

½ cup canned pumpkin

4 oz cream cheese

1 cup plain Greek yogurt

½ teaspoon freshly grated nutmeg

½ teaspoon cinnamon

½ teaspoon allspice

½ teaspoon sea salt

¼ teaspoon pure vanilla extract

1 tablespoon honey

1 Put pumpkin in food processor with cream cheese and blend until smooth.

2 In a bowl, mix together pumpkin and cream cheese with the rest of the ingredients and stir until thoroughly combined. Let chill. Serve with gingersnaps and graham crackers.

Lemon Curd

Serve this tart and whimsical curd with scones and mini cakes during afternoon tea! This curd can also be topped with meringue and put under a broiler to make lemon meringue pie.

1 Mix all ingredients in a stand mixer until well combined. Pour into saucepan and cook over low heat until thickened (approximately 10 minutes).

2 Pour into serving dish and let chill until thickened further. Serve with fruit, gingersnaps, and graham crackers.

INGREDIENTS:

½ cup freshly squeezed lemon juice, from 3–4 lemons

2 teaspoons lemon zest

3 large eggs

⅔ cup sugar

1 stick butter

Yogurt and Pistachio Dip

ACTIVE TIME: 10 MINUTES • TOTAL TIME: 10 MINUTES • SERVING SIZE: 2 CUPS

Reminiscent of pistachio ice cream, this scrumptious dip is best served with pizzelles, gingersnaps, or apple slices.

INGREDIENTS:

1 cup shelled pistachios

3 tablespoons butter

16 oz plain Greek yogurt

2 tablespoons honey

1 teaspoon cinnamon

½ teaspoon freshly grated nutmeg

1 In a food processor, blend pistachios and butter until a smooth paste forms. It should look something like almond or peanut butter.

2 Stir together pistachio mixture, Greek yogurt, honey, and spices until blended. Serve with apples, pears, and ginger snaps.

Chocolate Hazelnut Dip

ACTIVE TIME: 15–20 MINUTES • TOTAL TIME: 20–30 MINUTES •
SERVING SIZE: 1–1½ CUPS

Better known as Nutella, this homemade version is 100 times more flavorful and enchanting.

1 Roast hazelnuts in the oven at 350 degrees Fahrenheit for 12–15 minutes. Let cool. Put cooled hazelnuts, sugar, and salt into food processor and blend until paste forms.

2 Meanwhile, use a double boiler to melt the chocolate. Boil ½ inch of water in a saucepan and set a bowl over it so that it doesn't touch the water. Add chocolate to bowl on top.

3 Once chocolate is melted, whisk in the butter and cream off of the heat. Then whisk in the hazelnut paste.

4 Once combined, let chill. Serve with fresh fruit, on pound cake, or spread on a piece of toast for a delicious breakfast.

INGREDIENTS:

2 cups hazelnuts

⅓ cup sugar

1 teaspoon sea salt

16 oz semi-sweet chocolate, chopped

1 stick butter

1 cup heavy whipping cream

Dippables

So now you have all of these dips prepared for your next party, but how will you scoop them up? Although I do enjoy the guacamole and the hummus by the spoonful, here are some crisp, fresh, salty, and sweet vehicles to streamline these dips into your guests' mouths! Never underestimate the importance of a strong, flavorful dippable. These fun chips, veggies, crisps, and sweets enhance the flavors of the dips you choose to enjoy them with. Happy Dipping!

Homemade Potato Chips

ACTIVE TIME: 5 MINUTES • TOTAL TIME: 20 MINUTES • SERVES 4–6 PEOPLE

Here is a healthier version to the classic deep fried potato chip.

1 Thinly slice the potatoes. Depending on your preference, cut them as thin or thick as you like. I try to cut them paper thin. Toss the slices in the oil and lay on a baking sheet in one layer. Bake at 400 degrees Fahrenheit for 12–15 minutes or until golden brown.

2 As soon as they come out of the oven, toss the potatoes in the salt. Serve warm.

Variation: If you want to try different variations of spices, try tossing the warm chips in:
- 1 teaspoon freshly ground black pepper
- 1 teaspoon chili powder
- 1 teaspoon fresh thyme
- 1 teaspoon ground cumin
- 1 teaspoon ground coriander
- 1 teaspoon fresh rosemary
- $1/2$ teaspoon onion powder
- $1/2$ teaspoon garlic powder
- 1 teaspoon old bay seasoning
- 1 teaspoon red chili flakes, or really anything you like

INGREDIENTS:

3 large Yukon gold potatoes

4 tablespoons olive oil

2 teaspoons sea salt

Purple Potato Chips

Purple potatoes are a fun alternative to the classic white or yellow. Make these to add a pop of color to the chip bowl!

INGREDIENTS:

3 large purple potatoes

4 tablespoons olive oil

2 teaspoons sea salt

1 Thinly slice the potatoes. Depending on your preference, cut them as thin or thick as you like. I try to cut them paper thin. Toss the slices in the oil and lay on a baking sheet in one layer. Bake at 400 degrees Fahrenheit for 12–15 minutes or until golden brown.

2 As soon as they come out of the oven, toss the potatoes in the salt. Serve warm.

Beet Chips

These deep ruby roots make for beautiful and delicious crisps.

1 Thinly slice the beets. Depending on your preference, cut them as thin or thick as you like. I try to cut them paper thin. Toss the slices in the oil and lay on a baking sheet in one layer. Bake at 400 degrees Fahrenheit for 12–15 minutes or until golden brown.

2 As soon as they come out of the oven, toss the beets in the salt. Serve warm.

INGREDIENTS:

4–5 fresh beets

4 tablespoons olive oil

2 teaspoons sea salt

Pita Chips

Dip these warm pita triangles in hummus or salsa for a nice added crunch to the dip.

INGREDIENTS:

4 fresh pita breads

2 tablespoons olive oil

2 teaspoons sea salt

1 Cut pita bread in half lengthwise. Then cut each pita into 6 triangles. Brush with olive oil and bake at 375 degrees Fahrenheit for 10–12 minutes or until crisp.

2 Remove from oven and toss with salt while warm.

Tortilla Chips

ACTIVE TIME: 5 MINUTES • TOTAL TIME: 20 MINUTES • SERVES 8–10 PEOPLE

These chips are the perfect vehicle to deliver salsa, guacamole, or sour cream right to your taste buds!

1 Cut tortillas into 6–8 triangles. Brush with vegetable oil and lay on a baking sheet in a single layer. Bake at 400 degrees Fahrenheit for 8 minutes, then flip the triangles. Bake for another 8 minutes or until they are crisp and golden brown.

2 Remove from oven and toss with salt while warm. Serve.

Variation: You can also toss with chili powder, lime, cumin, coriander, paprika, cayenne pepper, or cinnamon sugar.

INGREDIENTS:

1 package corn tortillas

2 tablespoons vegetable oil

2 teaspoons sea salt

Crostini

These are a kitchen essential. Cut the baguette on a diagonal for a professional looking crostini.

INGREDIENTS:

1 baguette

¼ cup olive oil

1 Cut baguette on a diagonal into $\frac{1}{2}$ inch slices. Brush with olive oil. Lay on a baking sheet in one layer. Bake at 375 degrees Fahrenheit for 5 minutes. Turn the bread. Bake for another 5 minutes or until lightly toasted.

2 Serve warm or at room temperature.

Variation: Below are a couple of easy, and tasty, variations:

• Rub with a fresh garlic clove and the open half of a fresh tomato, sprinkle with lemon juice, and dust with cayenne pepper for a kick.

• Grill the bread for an added smoky flavor.

• Use different kinds of bread to make variations of the crostini. Try pumpernickel, whole wheat, rye, multigrain, cinnamon raisin, bagels, brioche, or challah.

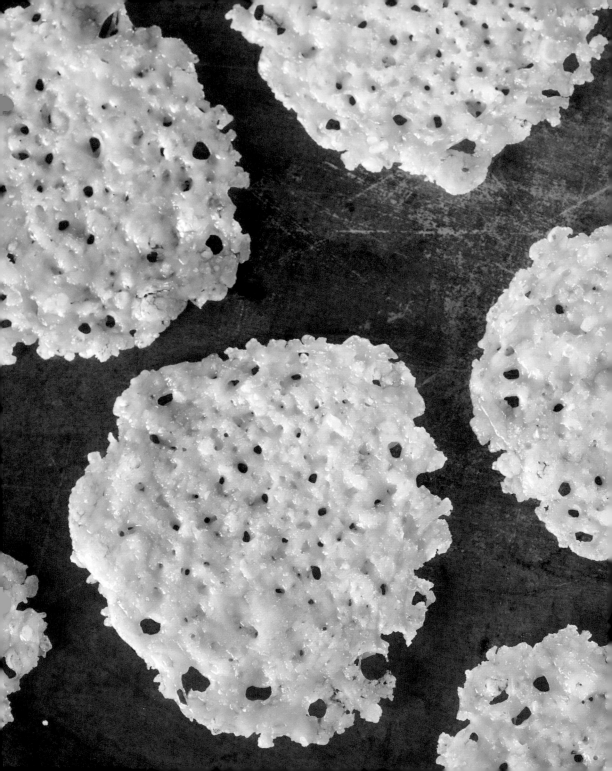

Parmesan Crisps

Top these crisps with bruschetta or Italian guacamole and see how the Parmesan adds a whole new level of flavor. These are also great on top of a salad!

Place 2 tablespoons of Parmesan onto a nonstick or silicone lined baking sheet. Bake at 400 degrees Fahrenheit for 4–6 minutes or until melted and lightly golden. Let cool and serve.

INGREDIENTS:

2 cups freshly grated Parmesan cheese

Homemade Crackers

ACTIVE TIME: 15 MINUTES • TOTAL TIME: 25–35 MINUTES • SERVES 8–10 PEOPLE

Homemade crackers are impressive yet always boring.

INGREDIENTS

1 cup all-purpose flour

4 tablespoons butter

2 teaspoons sea salt,
divided in half

¼ cup half and half

1 teaspoon black pepper

1 teaspoon poppy seeds

1. Combine flour, butter, and salt in a food processor until the mixture forms all together. Slowly start adding the half and half until mixture holds together.

2. Lay out a piece of wax paper and flour and knead the surface. Roll dough to approximately ⅛-inch thick.

3. Cut into strips or cracker shapes and place on a baking sheet.

4. Sprinkle with black pepper and sea salt, remaining poppy seeds. Bake at 400 degrees for 10–15 minutes or until golden brown.

Turnip Chips

Dip these in tzatziki or onion dip for a nice alternative to classic potato chips.

Thinly slice the turnips. Depending on your preference, cut them as thin or thick as you like. I try to cut them paper thin. Toss the slices in the oil and lay on a baking sheet in one layer. Bake at 400 degrees Fahrenheit for 12–15 minutes or until golden brown.

As soon as they come out of the oven, toss the turnips in the salt and serve.

INGREDIENTS:

3 large turnips

4 tablespoons olive oil

2 teaspoons sea salt

Prosciutto Crisps

ACTIVE TIME: 3 MINUTES • TOTAL TIME: 15–18 MINUTES • SERVES 4–6 PEOPLE

You won't need to dip these in anything! Serve with Swiss fondue or fresh bruschetta.

INGREDIENTS:

20 slices of prosciutto

Lay flat on a sheet pan in one layer. They will shrink, so you can put them pretty close together. Bake at 400 degrees Fahrenheit for 12–15 minutes or until golden brown and crispy.

Rice Crackers

These rice crackers are a great gluten-free alternative to the everyday cracker.

INGREDIENTS:

1–1¼ cups rice flour, may vary depending on consistency of dough

¾ teaspoon sea salt

2 tablespoons butter, melted

⅓ cup cold water

Sea salt and butter for top of cracker

1 In a food processor, pulse together flour, salt, and butter. After a few pulses, start streaming in the water. Do this slowly to ensure the dough forms correctly. Let processor run until the dough turns onto a ball. As soon as this happens, take the dough out of the food processor and place onto floured surface to roll out.

2 Roll dough as thin as you can without tearing. Sprinkle extra flour on surface and dough if the dough starts to stick.

3 Once rolled out, cut the dough into 2 inch circles, and lay flat on baking sheet. Brush top with melted butter and sprinkle with sea salt. Bake at 325 degrees Fahrenheit for 15–20 minutes or until crackers are lightly golden ground. Serve!

Chocolate-Covered Pretzels

ACTIVE TIME: 10–15 MINUTES • TOTAL TIME: 1 HOUR+ • SERVES 4–6 PEOPLE

Whether you choose to use pretzel rods or twists, these little treats are perfect for dipping in any of the dessert dips.

INGREDIENTS:

2 cups semi-sweet chocolate chips

1 tablespoon butter

20 long pretzel sticks or 50 classic pretzel twists

1 Place chocolate in microwave safe bowl. Microwave on high in 15 second intervals until chocolate is melted. Be sure to check after each time to ensure you don't overcook the chocolate—overcooked chocolate seizes. You want the melted chocolate to look glossy and smooth. Add the butter and stir until combined.

2 Dip pretzels in chocolate so they are coated in chocolate. Lay on a baking sheet lined with wax paper. Once all pretzels are covered, place the baking sheet in the fridge for an hour or more to let the chocolate set. Serve!

Chocolate-Covered Graham Crackers

ACTIVE TIME: 10–15 MINUTES • TOTAL TIME: 1 HOUR+ • SERVES 4–6 PEOPLE

To make indoor s'mores, try dipping these graham crackers in the marshmallow fluff dip!

Place chocolate in microwave safe bowl. Microwave on high in 15-second intervals until chocolate is melted. Be sure to check after each time to ensure you don't overcook the chocolate—overcooked chocolate seizes. You want the melted chocolate to look glossy and smooth. Add the butter and stir until combined.

Dip the graham crackers in chocolate so they are coated halfway in chocolate. Lay on a baking sheet lined with wax paper. Once all crackers are covered, place the baking sheet in the fridge for an hour or more to let the chocolate set. Serve!

Variation: Use 20 ginger snaps instead of the graham crackers.

INGREDIENTS:

2 cups semi-sweet chocolate chips

1 tablespoon butter

10 graham crackers, broken in quarters (most are perforated so this should be simple)

Roasted Shrimp

Perfect for a party! Serve with cocktail sauce, avocado crema, or chipotle and adobo sauce.

INGREDIENTS:

2 pounds fresh, shelled shrimp

3 tablespoons olive oil

2 teaspoons sea salt

2 teaspoons freshly ground black pepper

1 teaspoon red chili flakes (optional)

1 Toss all the ingredients in a large bowl until all the shrimp are evenly coated.

2 Lay the seasoned shrimp on a baking sheet in one even layer. Bake shrimp at 400 degrees Fahrenheit for 9–10 minutes. Serve warm or at room temperature.

Grilled Chicken Skewers

ACTIVE TIME: 25–30 MINUTES • TOTAL TIME: 25–30 MINUTES • SERVES 8–10 PEOPLE

These are superb with the peanut satay sauce!

1 Toss all ingredients in a bowl until chicken is evenly seasoned.

2 Skewer the chicken onto either metal or bamboo skewers so that they are secure. If using bamboo skewers, be sure to soak them in water for at least an hour before grilling. This will help the skewers avoid burning too fast.

3 Grill the chicken skewers over medium high heat until they are cooked through, approximately 4–5 minutes per side. Serve.

INGREDIENTS:

15 chicken tenders, or 4 medium chicken breasts sliced into strips

2 teaspoons sea salt

2 teaspoons freshly ground black pepper

1 lemon, juiced

4 tablespoons olive oil

1 teaspoon red chili flakes

Grilled Shrimp Skewers

ACTIVE TIME: 25–30 MINUTES • TOTAL TIME: 25–30 MINUTES • SERVES 8–10 PEOPLE

Enjoy these shrimp skewers with homemade cocktail sauce or tzatziki at your next summer BBQ!

INGREDIENTS:

1½–2 pounds shrimp, peeled and deveined

1 teaspoon paprika

2 teaspoons sea salt

2 teaspoons freshly ground black pepper

1 lemon, juiced

4 tablespoons olive oil

1 teaspoon red chili flakes

1 Toss all ingredients in a bowl until shrimp is evenly seasoned.

2 Skewer the shrimp onto either metal or bamboo skewers so that they are secure. If using bamboo skewers, be sure to soak them in water for at least an hour before grilling. This will help the skewers avoid burning too fast.

3 Grill the shrimp skewers over medium high heat until they are cooked through, approximately 4–5 minutes per side. Serve.

Cheese Twists

ACTIVE TIME: 15-20 MINUTES • TOTAL TIME: 30 MINUTES • SERVES 12-15 PEOPLE

These dippables will please all guests at your next party!

Roll out puff pastry on board until it is approximately 10 inches x 12 inches.

Combine all three cheeses, pepper, and thyme in a bowl.

Beat egg in a small bowl to make an egg wash. Lightly brush each pastry with the egg wash. This will act as a glue for the toppings. Then, sprinkle half of the cheese mixture onto the surface of each pastry, and light press into pastry.

Cut pastry into long strips and twist each strip. Then, place on baking sheet. Bake at 375 degrees Fahrenheit for 12-15 minutes or until twists are golden brown. Turn over each pastry and let finish cooking for 2-3 more minutes. Remove from oven and let cool on cooling rack. Serve!

INGREDIENTS:

2 sheets puff pastry, thawed

cup fontina cheese, grated

cup gruyere cheese, grated

cup Parmesan cheese, grated

teaspoon fresh thyme, minced

teaspoon freshly ground black pepper

1 egg

Cinnamon Twists

This recipe results in a perfect dipper for whipped cream or chocolate hazelnut dip!

INGREDIENTS:

2 sheets puff pastry, thawed

1 cup sugar

3½ tablespoons cinnamon

1 teaspoon freshly ground nutmeg

1 egg

1 Roll out puff pastry on board until it is approximately 10 inches x 12 inches.

2 Combine the sugar, cinnamon, and nutmeg in a bowl.

3 Beat egg in a small bowl to make an egg wash. Lightly brush each pastry with the egg wash. This will act as a glue for the toppings. Then, sprinkle half of the sugar mixture onto the surface of each pastry, and light press into pastry.

4 Cut pastry into long strips and twist each strip. Then, place on baking sheet. Bake at 375 degrees Fahrenheit for 12–15 minutes or until twists are golden brown. Turn over each pastry and let finish cooking for 2–3 more minutes. Remove from oven and let cool on cooling rack. Serve!

Crudité

Crisp vegetables are fantastic dippables when it comes to dips and salsa. Whichever combination you choose to make up your crudité platter, you can be sure they will hold up to the thickest of dips. Try to choose the vegetables that are in season so the flavors are maximized.

- Cucumber
- Carrot
- Radish
- Cherry tomato
- Red bell pepper
- Green bell pepper
- Broccoli
- Cauliflower
- Sugar snap peas
- Jicama
- Celery
- Endive spears

Index

ABOUT CIDER MILL PRESS BOOK PUBLISHERS

Good ideas ripen with time. From seed to harvest, Cider Mill Press brings fine reading, information, and entertainment together between the covers of its creatively crafted books. Our Cider Mill bears fruit twice a year, publishing a new crop of titles each spring and fall.

501 Nelson Place
Nashville, Tennessee 37214

cidermillpress.com